Kindergarten Chef

Kindergarten Chef

by Miss Wenthen's Students

Illustrated by Haru Wells

DODD, MEAD & COMPANY · NEW YORK

ISBN: 0-396-07014-0
Library of Congress Catalog Card Number: 74-7772
Printed in the United States of America

Teacher's Note

Here are the favorite dishes of my kindergarten chefs. Each a singular disciple of the art. And be he a Beard or be she a Child, all are represented by at least one specialty. A word of caution, however. No recipe has yet been tested by anybody over five years old. Though we're happy to report that every preparation has been unanimously awarded the Jefferson School Seal of Good Eating. Bon appétit!

MAUREEN WENTHEN

Contents

9

Alphabet Soup

BY RANDY DUBNO

Get letters any kind.
Take some water.
Put it in with the letters.

Let it cook and put some more water in it and
add vegetables: carrots, beans, corn, peas, chocolate chips, peanuts. Add some more water,
put into it 8 chickens and potatoes.
Cook it for 10 hours at 5 degrees.

11

Bacon and Eggs

BY CAROL RUDDY

Put 15 pieces of bacon,
and 16 eggs in a pan.

Cook for 15 minutes at 16 degrees, then eat!

Chicken

BY DOREEN SIMON

Make the skin.
Add meat.
Put in a bone.

Cook for 15 minutes at 5 degrees.

Chocolate Chip Cookies

BY CAROLYN SCHWARZLER

2 sticks of butter
Chocolate chips
Baking soda
3 cups of sugar

Mix it together, then put in a pan in oven for 3 hours at 3 degrees.

Carrots

BY LIZA PASSANTINO

Take 1 carrot, cut it up, put it in a pan in the oven for 3 hours at 3 degrees.

Peppermint Cake

BY TEDDY FRANZ

1 cup of pepper
White filling
Cherries
Green sprinkles

Put in oven 2 hours at 1,000,000 degrees.

Apple Pie

BY RONNIE PATTERSON

5 apples
Little sugar
Some water
5 teaspoons milk
2 cups of butter

Mix it up then bake at 10,000 degrees, then put
crust in the middle, then you're done.

Crabs

BY CHERYL BENSON

Take 5 crabs.
Tie their legs together and put cotton in their mouth. Put in a pot so they won't move or yell. Then you cook them for 4 hours at 2 degrees.

Cinnamon Cake

BY BRIAN WILD

1 cup flour
3 cups vanilla

Put this into a pan.
Put some more batter in it over 1 cup of cinnamon, then put more cinnamon on the top, about 1 cup.
Bake it about 15 minutes at 5 degrees.
Put white icing on it when you're finished.

Hamburgers

BY TRACEY MUSARRA

6 cups of flour
3 pounds of yeast
2 cups vanilla
13 cups of meat

Put on stove and cook for 15 minutes.

Dog Bones

BY KEVIN DUFFUS

Get some crumbs.
A bowl
Sticking juice

Put the crumbs in the bowl and then make it
into the shape of a dog bone, add sticking juice,
put it in the oven for 3 hours at 7 degrees.
Take it out of the oven and then you draw a
dog on it.
Then you give it to your dog.

People don't eat dog bones.

Hot Dogs

BY ROBYN BARNETT

Put some oil in and stir it up, then put some cream in it, then peaches, then chocolate cream, then vanilla cream, mix it all together and it turns into a hot dog.

Rice

BY LAUREN CURDGEL

Put beans in the oven, let it cook for 10 minutes and then put gravy on it.

Ice Cream Cake

BY SUSAN MUTSCHLER

1 dish of ice cream (any flavor)

Get a cake mix out.

Put the cake mix in the oven for 5 hours at 7 degrees.

Take it out and put it in a bowl.

Stuff the ice cream in it.

Get whipped cream, put it on the cake. Put cherries on it.

Then you're done.

Jello

BY STEVEN CORSI

Get a dish and put red stuff in it, put a box of
jello in it, then water, add whipped cream, wait
till stiff, hot it before you put it in refrigerator.

Lobster

BY KRISTINE RANUSKA

Crab gravy
Some plain meat
Strawberry sauce

Stir it up and then you pour it in a pan, put some shell on top of it, cook it for 8 minutes at 60 degrees.

Ice Cream

BY MICHAEL KNARRE

Chocolate
Vanilla

Mix it up and put in the freezer for 3 hours at
4 degrees.

Birthday Cake

BY LOUIS IANNANTUANO

Take some chocolate powder and cherries, and 2 cups of sugar and a pinch of water, put candles in it.
Bake it for 5 minutes at 60 degrees.

Macaroni

BY ERIC SWENSEN

Buy macaroni.
Ride home.

Cook it, put in a pot for 5 hours. Then you put
them in an oven at 5 degrees, put cheese on it,
then eat it.

Turkey

BY DEBBIE GRODEWALD

You need a turkey—10 inches long

Cook in oven for 12 minutes, put butter on it.
Put in 2 pounds of stuffing.
Cook it at 10 degrees.

Cherry Pie

BY PATRICIA O'LEARY

9 cherries
Some flour
3 pounds of sugar

Put crust on top of it and under it.
Then put it in the oven for 9 minutes at 12 degrees.
Then you take it, put it into a box, and then you sell it.

Chicken

BY LAUREN CURDGEL

Put oil in the oven, and a chicken (dead). Then you put oil on it and some more oil, put sugar on it, bake at 40 degrees for 3 minutes, then eat it.

Mashed Potatoes

BY RENE GRASSO

1 spoon of sugar
2 cups of butter
A little cream
Some water

Put it in the oven for ½ hour at 10 degrees, take it out and put more sugar on it, and eat it up.

Mini-Ravioli

BY KEVIN DUFFUS

Get some spaghetti.
Put meat in it.
Cook it.
Put Ragu sauce on it.
Eat it now, I think?

Donuts

BY STACEY ERICHSEN

4 cups of vanilla
4 pounds of sugar
1 cup butter

Mush the butter.
Put in 2 cups of milk, mix it all up.
Then you add 3 eggs in the bowl.
Mix it all up again, make it into a circle.
Put it in the oven for 15 minutes at 3 degrees.
When it is finished, put a hole in the middle
with hole puncher.

35

Milk

BY THERESA CERAVOLO

Take the milk from the hose on the cow.
Put it in a gallon jug.
Then you send it to the store.
Sell it to people for money.

Oatmeal Cookies

BY KIMBERLEY QUINN

A cup of oatmeal
2 cups of flour

Cook for two hours at any degrees you want!

Orange Juice

BY ANDREA HORVATH

Fly to Florida.
Take some oranges.
Squeeze them.
Then you mix it.
Then you shake it.
Pour it in a container and freeze it for 10 hours
at 2 degrees.

Pancakes

BY LOUIS IANNANTUANO

1 teaspoon of oil
A little water

Put a pancake in and bake at 6 degrees for 20 minutes.

Peanut Butter Balls

BY KATHY JAMIESON

4 jars peanut butter
Chocolate chips

Mix it up and then put evaporated milk in it. Stir it again and then roll it into a ball and then put more peanut butter in it, freeze it, flat it down, put more peanut butter in and freeze it. It turns into chocolate chip cookies and they are very tasty.

Fish

BY ERIC SWENSEN

Try to catch them out of the water.
Put them in a basket.
Add salt, pepper.
Put in the oven for 2 or 3 minutes at 7 degrees.

Chicken Parmesan

BY EVAN CALLAHAN

Get any chicken.
Stuff it with bread.
Put red stuff around it and any kind cheese.
Put it in the oven.

Cook for 600 hours at 0 degrees.

Peas

BY KRISTINE RANUSKA

1 cup of sugar
1 cherry

Cook at 4 degrees for 3 hours.

Chicken Chow Mein

BY LIZA PASSANTINO

A little soy sauce
10 cups of rice
Cooked chicken, 4 or 5 chickens cut them up
(no eyes, ears, or fingers)
Add 4 carrots.

Mix it all together and cook for 6 hours at 1
degree.

Duck

BY JOHN GAUGHAN

Get some stuffing.
Boil it in a pot with water.
Take the duck out of the freezer and wait 20 minutes and then you take the skin and put stuffing inside the skin and put it on the duck. Put sauce and cook it for 5 minutes at 40 degrees.

Hamburgers

BY CAROLYN SCHWARZLER

Hamburger meat.
Hit it, put it in the pan, then melt the cheese
on the hamburger then put ketchup and salt
and pepper. Then you are all done.

Potato Salad

BY HAROLD FARROW

Take 4 potatoes
Cut them up.
Add cherries.
Put 1 onion in it.
Add 1 gallon of vinegar and 1 pound of mayonnaise.

Mix it all up and then get out a fork and eat it.

Pumpkin Pie

BY EVAN CALLAHAN

Take some crust, and 3 sliced pumpkins.
Take some flour and put it on the pumpkins.
Put the pumpkins inside the crust and bake it
in the oven at 6 degrees for 10 minutes.
Eat it when it is done.

Take a pot any size, any color, and put the
leftovers in that for the next night.

Hot Dogs

BY STEVEN CORSI

Put water in a pan and 15 hot dogs.
Add ketchup.
Add sauerkraut.
Add milk.
Put on a stove.

Cook at 300 degrees for 16 hours, put in a bag
and then place in a freezer, take it out when
you want to eat it.

Ravioli

BY BRIAN WILD

 2 pounds of cheese
32 pounds of meat

Put it into a pot, add noodles.
Put gas under it at 1,000 degrees for 5 minutes.
Put it in a bottle on the shelf.
Then at lunch time take it off the shelf and eat it.

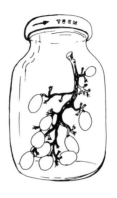

Jelly

BY KATHY JAMIESON

10 grapes

Put them in a pot—boil them.
Stir it, then put it in a jar.
Put it in the freezer for 10 minutes at 600
degrees.

Salad

BY TIMOTHY HOYT

Put some lettuce in, then vinegar and oil then
freeze it for 5 minutes at 6 degrees.

Spaghetti

BY JOEY TUCCINO

Take it out of the box.
Cook the spaghetti and crack it for a few
minutes.
Then you get a big plate and take it out of
the pot.
Put red sauce on it.
Then you eat.
Then wash the dishes.

Spare Ribs

BY THERESA GORMAN

Take some meat.
Get a bone.
Get elmer's glue and glue the meat on the bone.
Take it and boil it.
Then you freeze for 2 minutes.
Then you take it out and make barbecue sauce.
4 cups soy sauce
8 cups ketchup
Put that on the meat, cook them on a barbecue
and then you're finished.

Strawberries

BY TEDDY FRANZ

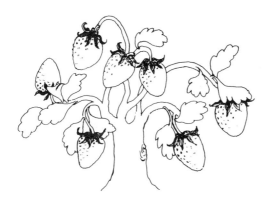

Grow a strawberry tree.
Then pick them off.

Put them in the oven at 4 degrees for 1 hour.
Take them out and then you eat them.

Strawberry Cake

BY KRISTINE RANUSKA

5 strawberries
1 teaspoon of water
2 cups sugar
Tomato sauce

Mix, then bake at 3 degrees, then put vanilla frosting and more sugar on it.

String Beans

BY MICHELLE GANNUCCI

Plant seeds.
Water them.
Pick them.

Then cook them in a pot for 10 minutes at 500
degrees.
Put salt on them, then eat them.

Turkey

BY MARK ADELHOCH

1 egg—put it in, this is the stuffing for a 3 foot turkey

Cook it for 40 hours at 16 degrees.
Then you dress it and sit down and eat.

Surprise Cake

BY ELIZABETH BARNETT

Crumbs and some smushed cookies

Add three sticks of butter and then squeeze it and then put it all in a big green bowl and then get some ice cream, toothpicks, and marshmallows.
Stick it all together and cook it for 10 hundred hours, put in a freezer for a few minutes, then you take it out and eat it.

Salad Dressing

BY RENE GRASSO

Put in 1 cup of milk.
2 cups of water
4 pounds of sugar

Cook it all up for 40 hours at 10 degrees.
Take it out and stir it up, wait till it smooths down, put in the refrigerator, and put in a salad dressing bottle. Then you put it on your salad.

Tomatoes

BY HENRY SO

Make a straight line.
Cut a circle.
Put red things in it.
Then you put spaghetti and meatballs in it,
then you eat.

Veal Cutlet

BY RANDI DUBNO

Make some dough.
Roll it.
Put crust on it.
Then put some meat on the top.
Put sugar on the meat, cook it for 10 minutes at 90 degrees.
Then take it out of the oven.

Tuna Fish Sandwich

BY TOMMY KRISTIANSEN

Take out a can of tuna fish—the tuna fish is 2 feet long, and you have to make him tiny to fit inside the can.
Take the tuna out of the can.
Mash it.
Add 2 pounds of mayonnaise.
Take 1 piece of bread, put it on the bread and then you eat it.

Hot Dogs

BY SUSAN MUTSCHLER

Take dough and smash it and roll it, cook it for 3 minutes at 4 degrees. Then take it out, put it on some bread, put ketchup on it and mustard and then you eat it. Tastes good.